When Your Proposal Author is AI

A Reference Guide for Proposal Editors
in the Age of AI Generative Content

Todd Hayes, Robert Thompson, and Jilian Peeke

When Your Proposal Author is AI

A Reference Guide for Proposal Editors in the Age of Generative Content

First Edition Paperback

This book is dedicated to Robert Thompson, our co-author and a brilliant writer of proposals and history books, who died shortly before we published.

Thank you, Bob, for your many years of service to the country, for your dedication to the projects we shared, and for being a good friend.

"By far, the greatest danger of artificial intelligence is that people conclude too early that they understand it."
Eliezer Yudkowsky

"We are a society strangling in unnecessary words, circular constructions, pompous frills and meaningless jargon."
William Zinsser

"It is perfectly okay to write garbage — as long as you edit brilliantly."
C.J. Cherryh

"Editing is the art of seeing the invisible."
Joyce Carol Oats

Table of Contents

Appendix 1. Proposal-specific AI Product Review (Proposal Pilot)

Appendix 2: Useful Resources

Appendix 3: Prompt Engineering Logic

Introduction

In late 2024, technical experts in the proposal writing industry were talking about how generative AI was going to change how we produce content within five years. We would be using intelligent software to ingest requirements and processes, analyze compliance, and auto-generate bids and content better and faster than humans could ever do it. These predictions are starting to come true, but instead of a five years it only took a few months.

The reason we all accepted that five-year forecast is that Request for Proposal (RFP) responses, especially related to government RFPs, have always been a monster effort. Large government bids (contracts worth $200M or more) historically involve hundreds of people, including niche solution experts, subject matter experts (SMEs), and techincal, management, and business leaders across departments. Proposal teams are staffed with managers, volume leads, writers, artists, editors, reviewers, and coordinators required to organize contributors, progress content, draft and review proposal products, and adapt to changing requirements under tight deadlines. With all the schedule and staffing contingencies, mistakes or setbacks at any level had consequences that were often painful to resolve.

By the beginning of 2025, we were hearing about the unreliability of generative AI. For most of us, our only long-term exposure to smart applications had been watching Autocorrect change the meaning of our texts right before we hit send, sometimes to our great embarrassment. We saw videos of AI fast food drive-thrus adding hundreds of chicken nuggets to a customer order. We saw NBA stars wrongly accused of vandalism (AI misinterpreted the term "throwing bricks"). We saw legal research teams accepting AI-fabricated court cases as truth. We saw social-media-trained AI churning racist and misogynistic posts. AI was misinterpreting instructions and recycling unrelated content as if it was relevant. AI was generating dorky metaphors, inserting em dashes in every sentence, and using clunky words such as "embark," "deep dive" and "delve.". The result was AI-generated material that didn't look like something a human would write.

We were right to be afraid and skeptical of this technology. But just like a human child, AI continues to mature through training and correction and the industry has already decided it's time for it to enter the workforce for real.

We created this handbook as a guide for proposal editors to help them alleviate the fears of working with generative AI during this machine adolescent period. This guide shows how to apply processes and training methods to reduce and catch errors while still realizing the time savings and organizational benefits driving its adoption. Many editors will have new tasks to add to their checklists. If you are accustomed to being integrated with the response team and heavily involved in compliance reviews, then the this will be an extension of what you already do, albiet with higher stakes and less room for error, because now you're not going to be sure where the content is coming from, or where the source data that built the content is coming from.

Our generation will likely never lose its suspicion of AI-generated content, no matter how good it gets. For now, that suspicion is a great asset for proposal preparation and editing.

What Is AI?

AI tools are programs that learn to create content through training on massive datasets called Large Language Models (LLMs), and they are rapidly changing the world. Generative AI can identify patterns and relationships and make their own conclusions, or they can develop conclusions based on a user's preferences. A user can enter prompts, direct them to source materials, set rules and priorities, and train them further to produce the desired content, from simple sentences to full reports and entire proposals. AI uses a set of rules and priorities to mimic a response and plug in the next word, the next idea, or the next image it expects will satisfy the objective.

Imagine you have just hired a super sharp college graduate, fresh out of school, with a phenomenal work ethic. Your new hire lacks industry experience related to your field and is a bit socially awkward, so you need to spend some quality time educating them, and you need to check their work carefully. They also never say, "I don't know how to do that." Instead, they give any task their best shot using whatever resources they find they think might help.

This is the same persona as a generative AI tool like ChatGPT.

LLMs like ChatGPT train on a massive amount of available content (such as artciles, books, websites, and public converstations) to predict the next word in a sentence. They are getting better and better at mimicking constructs, images, and narratives based on what they've learned, but they only know what they are fed. The trouble is, we don't always know where the information is originating with an LLM unless we are dilligent in customizing it for our purposes. The assumptions the model can make based on biased, incorrect, or halucinated data pose a threat to our RFP response outputs.

Why Proposal Editors Matter More Than Ever in the Age of AI

The AI-authored proposal has arrived suddenly. Generative AI tools like ChatGPT, Claude, and Gemini are now embedded into the workflows of proposal professionals. AI tools have several benefits. They can:

- Reduce production time, eliminate writer's block, and provide 24/7 support

- Ingest and transform large amounts of data instantly

- Create their own claims and arguments

- Recall details across documents

- Suggest new types of artifacts to support your mission

- Receive corrections without having hurt feelings

For proposal managers facing impossible deadlines and limited resources, the arrival of AI may feel like a blessing, but there are blind spots and "gotchas" living in this new territory that one must address. Assuming that any content generated automatically is good-to-go is a mistake that could have long-lasting consequences, including damage to your firm's reputation.

AI-generated content can suffer from vague language, missing context, repetitive sentence structures, hallucinated facts, inappropriate examples and metaphors, and a misaligned tone. These tools may be able to structure a persuasive

In the case of _Mata v. Avianca Inc._, the U.S. District Court for the Southern District of New York sanctioned a law firm for submitting a briefing generated by ChatGPT that quoted completely fabricated cases as precedent.

This widely publicized event has inspired many discussions on the responsible use of AI to generate content, especially when there are legalities involved.

paragraph, but they don't inherently understand government acquisition rules, compliance checklists, content priorities, industry nuances, or your customer's evaluation logic. Moreover, readers and evaluators can tell when something has been fully produced by AI, and they often have an immediate visceral and negative reaction to it. This, of course, can have very adverse implications for a company's probability of winning (PWin). That's why the human proposal editor has recently received a promotion to a supervisory role over the new AI workforce.

The modern proposal editor has become the quality assurance gatekeeper for identifying erroneous data, policing automated fluff, and ensuring content relevance. They must not only identify where the language fails, but also determine why it failed, how to fix it, and how to prevent the issue next time by training the AI differently.

This process includes making the AI-generated material sound less formulaic and more human. The effort required to accomplaish this should not be understimated. Making AI sound more human can require just as much thinking and creativity as writing the entire proposal yourself if your AI tool is not learning to adjust course and fix mistakes as you go.

How to Use This Guide

This handbook is about how to edit proposals that have been written using AI tools in whole or in part so they are stronger, cleaner, smarter, and safer to submit. We must approach editing as a mission-critical function when content is being generated by tools that don't fully understand the business, the buyer, or the win strategy.

You'll learn how to evaluate structure, verify facts, shape tone, enforce compliance, and improve cross-volume consistency. Each chapter is a practical guide to one aspect of proposal editing, including step-by-step checklists and AI training tips for ChatGPT. You'll come away with a playbook you can use on any federal, state, or commercial proposal.

You can use this handbook as a solo reference or as a team resource. Each checklist can be adapted into a task sheet or integrated into your internal review cycle. Many of the AI tips are designed to be reused in prompt libraries, giving you tools to improve your AI's behavior over time. For teams managing revision logs or style guide enforcement, the checklists can also double as internal QA metrics.

AI engineering is evolving rapidly. Large firms who began in-house AI development years ago are now on their second and third generation of custom AI. Some are using context engineering and memory, as opposed to prompt engineering, to enable better results. New applications and generative methods are emerging every week. **Because of this we are limiting training tips to ChatGPT** prompt examples as it is the most common tool for beginners. Other AI tools will likely morph, evolve, combine, and disappear in the months and years ahead.

If your firm is using a closed system for its own custom AI tool, you may not need to worry about security breaches due to AI sharing proprietary data externally. But if you're using any version of ChatGPT, *you must setup the AI so it does not share your data with the world.*

How to Disable Data Sharing Through ChatGPT Settings (Important!)

If you do not disable data sharing while working with ChatGPT, your content can end up as part of the pool of knowledge that OpenAI uses as source material. This can pose a significant threat to security or privacy when dealing with any classified, proprietary, or personal information. ChatGPT has an option for disabling data sharing.

To disable data sharing in ChatGPT go to your account **Settings** and select **Data Controls**. Find **Improve the model for everyone** at the top and turn this option to OFF.

When working with sensitive information you should also submit a Privacy Request by going to the OpenAI Privacy Policies page (https://privacy.openai.com/policies) and request that ChatGPT not train on the content you are working on.

If your organization does not yet have an AI component in their privacy policy to protect your corporate, client, or personnel data, now is a great time to add it.

Chapter 1: Editing the Outline

Ensuring Logic, Flow, and Evaluator Readability

A strong outline sets the stage for persuasive content, win theme placement, and provides evaluator-friendly navigation. Typically, a proposal manager or writer creates the proposal outline corresponding to the RFP requirements in anticipation of the government's scoring process. We want to address all the requirements an evaluator will score in the document in a logical place where they won't be missed.

For federal procurements, there are three elements at a minimum needed to build the proposal outline:

1) The proposal instructions of a solicitation (traditionally in Section L) usually outline the major order and structure of the response. Section L either states directly or references the requirements to address in the response.

2) The proposal evaluation criteria (traditionally in Section M) explain how evaluators will score the response.

3) The statement of work (SOW) or performance work statement (PWS) (traditionally in Section C or provided as an attachment to the RFP) details requirements and work efforts for the project at hand.

When building a response outline, the proposal manager (PM), proposal writer, or compliance editor usually begins with Section L instructions to map and number the outline in the proper order, including volumes, sections, and subsections. With any luck, the RFP has been numbered in a way that can carry over to the response outline, which makes it clearer which sections of the response map to the RFP.

Next, according to the references in Section L, the PM or writer maps the evaluation criteria from Section M and requirements from Section C (requirements referenced in Section L) into the response outline. Section L may also refer to other proposal sections, appendices, or requirements and processes not included in the RFP that you need to integrate into the outline to make sure you address all scorable areas.

Finally, an outline needs to accommodate placement for your win themes (team strengths and discriminators) and client benefits.

There are now several applications that can help you draft your outline. Document parsing and extraction tools such as Diffbot, Rossum, and Grooper automate the reading and structuring of complex RFPs, helping identify requirements, dates, clauses, and compliance risks. This list of tools is likely to grow and become more sophisticated as AI capabilities are increasing logarithmically across multiple industries. Even ChatGPT can create a good response outline for you if you feed it the RFP and give it instructions on how to prioritize and return content. If you feed the AI previous proposals (that were compliant and compelling) with relevant data or other deal strategy documents, it can even recommend win themes and client benefits that are applicable to the project at hand.

At first glance, an AI-generated proposal outline may appear structured and professional, but we can't assume this draft is strategically sound, or that it properly covers all the requirements necessary to present a compliant and compelling response. Unlike a human author, AI does not "think like an evaluator" unless you specifically train it to do so. It may generate repetitive or awkward hierarchies, mislabel sections, or distribute content unevenly.

As the editor, you must review the structure against the RFP for compliance alignment, strategic positioning, and content coverage. There may also be mistakes, omissions, or contradictory requirements in the RFP (especially in a pre-final draft) that an AI won't know how to catch. The outline editor needs to assess the entire outline for the following six topics before distributing a template to authors or SMEs for drafting sections, or before sending it back to the AI to create a first draft. Each chapter of this guide parses these topics as actions in a Quality Checklist.

1. Compliance Alignment

Does the outline follow the order of instructions and evaluation criteria in the RFP?

When reviewing an AI-generated outline, your first job as editor is to check whether it matches the structure dictated by the RFP. This means aligning to both Section L (Instructions) and Section M (Evaluation Criteria) and incorporating requirements from other sections as instructed by Section L. Many AI tools default to writing in generic narrative form or use templates learned from prior prompts and training, which can result in structures that feel plausible but diverge from the solicitation at hand.

Learning and retaining that learning is a key shortcoming of AI tools. An August 2025 Massachusetts Institute of Technology (MIT) Networked Agents and Decentralized AI (NANDA) report found that 95% of businesses' generative AI pilots are failing to get a measurable return on investment (ROI). The report found that the core barrier to scaling is not infrastructure, regulation, or talent. Rather, the biggest barrier to effective AI was learning. Most AI systems are struggling to retain feedback, adapt to context, or improve over time. This can cause problems in creating a compliant and responsive proposal using AI.

An outline may appear beautifully logical, but if it doesn't directly trace the evaluator's roadmap, you're asking to lose points. Check for re-ordered sections, collapsed headings, or invented labels. Evaluators follow a very specific sequence when scoring, and if your outline doesn't follow that path, the proposal risks appearing non-compliant.

Look for additional requirements that need to be addressed. For example, Section L may refer to a Section C requirement that references an appendix item that points to a Federal standard document this is not included in the RFP materials. Section M may have additional evaluation criteria that doesn't map naturally into the Section L outline, so it must be included strategically using keywords that the evaluator can find. Once you identify keywords or requirements that are missing from your outline, you can use your AI to help find similar omissions.

2. Content Coverage

Are any major RFP requirements or evaluation factors missing or underrepresented?

AI can sometimes miss the forest for the trees. The outline may skip entire sections of the RFP. It may also combine unrelated items under a single heading, assuming they are conceptually similar. Editors must verify that every required volume, section, and subtask in the instructions and evaluation criteria is represented in the outline in the proper order. This includes appendices, annexes, and sections for pricing, staffing, or security sections the AI might overlook because it doesn't immediately understand the relevance or nuance of the ask.

Also pay close attention to subsection parsing. For example, if the RFP asks for a Staffing Plan with five distinct components, the outline should reflect all five areas, as they will be scored individually. Building a cross-reference compliance matrix of the outline using the RFP's requirement language will help writers (including AI writers) to stay on track later in the process.

3. Contradictions in the RFP Instructions or Requirements

Do we need clarification from the contracting office that issued the RFP?

Many government solicitations contain internal contradictions, such as referring to a section or requirement that doesn't exist, listing a position in the technical response that doesn't align with the business volume, or even language copied from another solicitation that just doesn't make sense in this one. Section L may ask you to explain your detailed plan to operate the government's existing technical environment without providing any detail on the government's tech stack already in place. Detecting these discrepancies early, when the outline is still forming, can save a lot of time and stress in the weeks to come.

Use margin notes or comment logs to flag potential conflicts between sections of the RFP, especially if changes can affect the overall outline or structure. Is there a requirement that seems out of scope? Are two similar instructions in different sections mutually exclusive? AI can easily miss these contradictions unless it's explicitly trained to compare sections side-by-side. Even then, it may not understand the implications. These are the types of questions that turn into clarification questions (Q&A) to submit to the contracting office.

4. Industry Terminology

Does the outline use terms from the RFP properly?

AI is good at mimicking jargon. It's not always good at using jargon correctly. AI sometimes invents its own interpreted headings and synonyms and can misuse government-specific terminology. For example, it may label a task "Approach to Contract Execution" when the RFP calls it "Program Implementation Strategy." These may seem like the same topic, but misalignment in terminology can signal potential non-compliance or cause evaluators to miss relevant content.

As the editor, your job is to ensure that terminology in the outline mirrors the RFP exactly when it comes to headings, processes, and technical references. Even informal terms like how the agency refers to its own mission, tools, or goals should be reflected in the outline. If the RFP says "Workstream," don't let AI call it a "Phase." These differences matter, especially to technical evaluators, and the RFP might use the word "phase" elsewhere in reference to something completely different.

5. Logical Subsection Flow

Does the response outline make sense from an evaluator's perspective?

A well-written outline is a roadmap that helps the evaluator understand the offeror's logic and approach according to their scoresheet. Ask yourself, if you were scoring this proposal as an evaluator, would the outline help or hinder your ability to do your job? A good outline makes the proposal easy to read and score.

Never assume that AI is the authority on any topic, especially an AI tool that hasn't been extensively trained on the exact subject matter. Look for section subcategories that feel bloated, redundant, or out of order. Sometimes AI will include three separate headings that all mean the same thing, introduce an appendix item in the body of the response, or pile in completely unrelated information based on some random association. Sometimes AI will skip subsections that are clearly an important part of the response.

If there is a redundancy in the RFP and a page limit, the right move is usually to leave the redundant subheading and create a cross reference that guides the evaluator to where the item is addressed thoroughly. AI won't know how to do this unless it is trained, and even then, you must quality check each cross-reference.

6. Strategic Positioning

Are win themes, differentiators, and benefits positioned early and reinforced throughout?

AI content can be generic and unnecessarily verbose. You need to prompt it to prioritize win themes and key ideas that differentiate your offer from competitors. An effective outline should provide room for win themes and team strengths as a regular part of the section structure.

As the editor, look for opportunities in the outline to front-load value, including:

- Section openers with one or more strategic client benefits

- Section-level callout boxes for past performance tie-ins and team strengths

- Places to highlight your unique tools or approaches

Strategic positioning statements can guide human writers and AI systems alike to create more persuasive, evaluator-focused content. When teams are thinking about win themes at the outline stage, the proposal will have mature strategic concepts by the time it's delivered.

7. Chapter 1 Quality Checklist: Editing the Outline

Use the following checklist to review the strength and effectiveness of an AI-generated outline:

- ☐ Confirm the outline mirrors the structure and order of Section L (Instructions) and Section M (Evaluation Criteria).

- ☐ Ensure all required volumes, sections, subsections, appendices, and references are present and mapped properly.

- ☐ Review subsection parsing: Each compound requirement (e.g., "will" or "shall statement") should be separated and labeled clearly.

- ☐ Check for missing content or underrepresented topics, especially from referenced documents, attachments, or Section C (SOW or PWS).

- ☐ Flag any contradictions or unclear references in the RFP that could impact the outline structure or section content.

- ☐ Ensure the RFP's terminology is used consistently (e.g., don't replace "Program Management Strategy" with "Execution Plan").

- ☐ Review the logical flow of sections and subsections—are topics easy for an evaluator to follow and score?

- ☐ Address any redundancies by preserving necessary headings and creating cross-references (especially for page-limited volumes).

- ☐ Identify areas to embed win themes, client benefits, and differentiators at the section or subsection level.

- ☐ Note required support inputs (SME, past performance, business, security, etc.) in outline comments to guide the drafting process.

- ☐ Add placeholders or annotations for obvious opportunities to use graphics, tables, and callout boxes aligned with the message strategy.

☐ Finalize version control process, authorship assignments, and outline distribution notes for the proposal team.

8. AI Training Tips: Teaching the AI to Create a Better Outline

You can help your AI generate smarter, more compliant outlines by improving the input and feedback loop. Prompts can be combined, but you will probably have better luck using them iteratively in the beginning as the AI trains as you go. You can keep the AI version as the master, or you can copy the AI's outline into your working document and then feed it back to the AI as the most recent updated version. Try using some of the following strategies and sample prompts as needed during your outlining task.

SETUP TIPS

- <u>Disable data sharing in ChatGPT: Go to your account settings/data controls and turn off "Improve the model for everyone."</u>

- Provide the AI with RFP context: Upload or paste in Section L, Section M, and relevant parts of Section C and major appendices.

- Clarify the objective: Tell the AI the outline will serve evaluators using scoring rubrics based on keywords from the RFP.

- Share past performance examples and relevant documents: Feed the AI prior outlines and their associated RFPs, existing win themes, or section structures from similar contracts, with instructions to mimic format, flow, tone, rationale, themes, format, etc. (but not requirements; requirements can only come from the current RFP).

PROMPT EXAMPLES

Basic Outline Prompt

Act as an expert proposal writer specializing in <<*insert subject matter or solicitation title*>>. Using the attached Section L and M from the RFP, generate a detailed response outline that mirrors the structure, preserves headings, and reflects evaluation priorities. Include numbered subsections where needed.

Evaluator Logic Prompt

Act as a federal evaluator using a checklist to score this proposal outline. The outline will serve evaluators using scoring rubrics based on keywords and requirements from the RFP. What outline structure would help you find and score the required elements efficiently?

Compliance Matrix Prompt

Map each item in Section L to its corresponding Section M evaluation criteria and organize the outline accordingly. Flag any items that don't appear to have a natural match.

Win Theme Integration Prompt

For each major section of the outline, recommend at least one win theme or client benefit that should be featured. These should reflect team strengths, differentiators, or low-risk/high-value claims. Any client benefit should reflect time saved, money saved, enhanced performance, or lower risk.

Terminology Guardrail Prompt

Do not substitute or paraphrase any headings or key terms from the RFP. Use exactly the same language from the RFP document to reference requirement key words unless instructed otherwise. The purpose of this is to ensure proper scoring by the evaluator.

FEEDBACK LOOP TIPS

After reviewing the AI-generated outline and finding issues, you can return comments that will help AI understand your priorities, such as:

- Reorder sections to match RFP Section L exactly and include a new section for <<*Appendix X*>>.

- For each section of the outline with headings 1, 2, or 3, include the numbered section from the RFP that the line item refers to.

- Add relevant win theme notes from the attached document "X" to the Technical Approach outline.

- Do not add icons when generating text. Use bold text for subheads. Do not use em dashes unless mimicking an RFP element that has an em dash.

- Include cross-references in the document for duplicate topics covered in multiple sections using an italic font style.

- Revise this outline based on the editor's feedback comments (attached) and update the structure accordingly. Keep all requirement numbers and section labels visible.

- Recommend areas in the response that would benefit from additional data expressed in tables or graphics.

Chapter 2: Editing the Solution

Verifying the Technical and Management Response Claims

AI-generated proposal content is often cleanly worded, grammatically sound, and organized. But that doesn't make it accurate, specific, or convincing. One of the most critical functions of the editor is to review the solution section—often the Technical Approach, Management Plan, or Implementation Strategy—to ensure that what's being promised is credible, tailored, and aligned with the customer's expectations.

This chapter guides editors through verifying whether the AI has offered a generic placeholder or a true solution grounded in contract reality. Inaccurate or oversimplified responses can create liability and break trust with the reviewer. Reviewers are looking for responses that demonstrate insight into the customer's needs, show how the offeror fulfills those needs, and make it clear why the approach is low-risk and high-value. AI won't do this without guidance.

1. Relevance and Specificity of the Solution

Does the solution address the solicitation requirements?

Start by checking if the proposed solution actually addresses requirements. AI can drift toward generic content, describing an ideal process or capability while ignoring the customer's specific context. If the RFP asks how you will staff a 24/7 help desk in multiple time zones, the response should mention time zones, help desk structure, and specifics about the shift rotation and service hours. Using "industry best practices for shift support" won't cut it.

Review the RFP SOW or PWS from Section C side-by-side with the solution documents. Mark any sections that feel vague or that could have been written for any contract. Ask yourself this question: Would this be impressive or useful to an evaluator familiar with the project, or does it feel like tangential information that may not be scorable? If the solution is touting a special process or asset that is not asked for in the requirements, it must be obvious to the evaluator which requirements it addresses and what customer benefits will be achieved from its use.

2. Technical Accuracy and SME Validation

Verify stated features with the experts.

Even when the language looks plausible, you must verify that the content is technically sound. Did AI invent a tool, process, or product name? Did it overpromise automation or include systems the company doesn't actually use?

As the editor, you should verify each tool or process mentioned is in scope for the proposal to determine if it is appropriate for the response. Verify with SMEs and leadership if the parts of the solution are accurate. Even with non-AI contributors, proposed tools and processes can slip into a response that have not been approved by company leadership, and sometimes not even priced for the bid. One software license for 1,000 users on a complex program can add millions of dollars to a bid, so these extra solution elements cannot be taken lightly.

Solution issues like these may not be caught by a proposal writer or SME working in isolation. Make sure you involve technical SMEs to review flagged areas before material is presented for review.

AI should never be the final authority for technical content. Look for any overconfident statements that imply compliance, innovation, or efficiency and assume that no one has verified the approach other than the AI author. As a best practice, keep a list of approved solution items including tools, processes, organization charts, roles and responsibilities matrices, and work schedules, and check them against current content.

3. Use of Operational Detail

Did we cover the HOW?

Proposal evaluators often give higher scores to responses that describe not only what the contractor will do, but how they will do it. Editors should look for operational details that make the solution believable and achievable. Instead of "we monitor performance metrics," it should say, "our project coordinator monitors performance using established metrics and generates monthly compliance dashboards using XYZ software, which the Program Manager reviews and submits to the Contracting Officer."

When AI glosses over "the how," it creates a weak spot. The editor's job is to make sure the writing includes enough detail to instill confidence without overwhelming the evaluator with irrelevant depth. If you have detailed solution data from the team, you can ask your AI to suggest how-statements that you can distribute appropriately by topic (see quality checklist below), including who, how, and when questions about the methodology.

Some of the content AI generates will be uninteresting or obvious, even when it is correct, and you'll want to cut it. Some content will totally miss the mark. Some AI details will provide additional value that the team hasn't defined appropriately. A good editor anticipates all these scenarios with AI-generated content, cuts or edits obvious fails, and asks team members to clarify and verify the approach when there's any doubt.

An AI-generated solution document may over focus on one area and ignore another that receives the same weight. When human writers do this, it's usually because they know that a relevant operational process has been covered in a previous section, and they just forgot to mention that the same process also applies to this other section. AI might just skip some essential information, seemingly lost in a tangential train of thought. It may also add pages and pages to an insignificant or irrelevant topic. The editor should ensure that response sections are evenly distributed and weighted according to the outline as they will be scored by an evaluator, unless leadership has specifically said to "beef up" a section because it's one of the greatest discriminators offered on the bid. AI should not be deciding on this weighting on its own.

4. Relationship to Customer Challenges

Are challenges stated, and does the customer care about them?

Look for sections that acknowledge customer pain points or project constraints. If the AI writes a technical section without referencing known customer priorities or past performance insights, it is an incomplete response. You may need to add framing sentences that the team has identified that speak to the customer's legacy systems, staffing gaps, transition risks, or audit requirements.

These adjustments don't always come from the RFP—they often come from capture intel, win themes, or incumbent knowledge. Sometimes challenges are stated in RFP introductions that need to be addressed throughout the response. AI won't know these unless fed directly, and even then, it may misinterpret the challenge or the associated mitigation.

AI may also take a challenge and embellish it dramatically without being prompted to do so. And it may borrow some other customer's challenge without permission. If you can't find their mention in the solicitation, check with the team to make sure that challenges stated are real for the customer and that any details about those challenges are not hallucinated or assumed.

5. Chapter 2 Quality Checklist: Editing the Solution

Use this checklist to identify weak spots and strengthen AI-generated content in the solution section:

- ☐ Confirm that the solution directly addresses each scoped requirement from Section C or its references in Section L.

- ☐ Flag any generic descriptions that could apply to any customer or contract as opposed to being specific to the current bid.

☐ Remove or revise any non-relevant or tangential content that cannot be scored according to RFP criteria.

☐ Identify and verify all product names, tools, systems, certifications, or approaches with SMEs.

☐ Check for missing operational detail—each action or claim should be described clearly in terms of "who does what, when, and how."

☐ Ensure the solution references customer-specific pain points, challenges, legacy systems, or stated evaluation preferences.

☐ Remove or revise any "overpromising" language that lacks evidence or feasibility.

☐ Insert calls for data, graphics, or references to case studies to support the approach where appropriate.

☐ Add section comments where SME input is required for technical details or verification.

☐ Check solution elements for staffing, scheduling, or tool references across Technical, Management, Staffing, and Business topics.

☐ Ensure any diagrams or tables mentioned are described accurately in the narrative and properly support the requirements at hand.

☐ Check for validity and embellishment of stated customer challenges.

6. AI Training Tips: Improving the Solution Draft

To get stronger solution content from AI tools like ChatGPT, apply these strategies and sample prompts.

SETUP TIPS

- Provide the RFP scope of work or Section C with highlighting on key requirements.

- Share internal capability documents or past project descriptions and give the AI known solution exceptions as they apply the current bid.

- Include known customer concerns or agency hot buttons.

- Attach win themes, transition strategies, or risk mitigation messages from your capture plan.

PROMPT EXAMPLES

Base Draft Prompt

Act as a proposal writer creating the Technical Approach section for <<*RFP Title*>>. Use Section C and known customer concerns (listed below) to draft a solution that is clear, detailed, and feasible. Avoid generic language. Highlight who does what, when, and how. Assume each 3rd level heading has equal scoring weight and should take similar page space in the response.

Operational Detail Prompt

Revise this solution draft to include operational details for each claim. If the draft says we manage risks, without providing detail, add how that will be done, by whom, and using what method or tool if known.

Verification Prompt

List all product names, tools, processes, and certifications referenced in this draft and compare it against our solution summary document. Highlight any items in the draft that need to be verified for accuracy to update the solution summary document.

Customer Focus Prompt

Rewrite the solution in section X so that it includes the customer's known pain points—such as <<*insert items*>>. Describe how our approach will help resolve those pain points and challenges.

Tool Comparison Prompt

Generate a comparison table of our proposed tool against the legacy tool currently used by the customer. Include features, implementation effort, and user experience benefits.

Chapter 3: Editing for Compliance

Reviewing the Must Haves: Mandatory Content, Order, and References

Compliance is the navigational constant that ensures your proposal content can be seen, scored, and accepted. AI can assemble a rudimentary proposal quickly, but it does not really understand the implicit logic and legal significance encoded within the structure of a government RFP. The editor's role is to verify that every element the evaluators seek is present, properly labeled, and in the correct place. This chapter defines the structures that govern compliance and how to uphold them with precision.

1. Mapping Content to the RFP Structure

Does the response outline follow Section L instructions?

Every federal solicitation provides a roadmap: Section L outlines the required structure and content of your response; Section M reveals the scoring logic; Section C describes the technical mission; and other sections (H, J, K, and beyond) may contain hidden mandates that need to be account for. Your job is to align these solicitation elements so that each response element lands precisely where the evaluator expects it and accounts for all requirements.

Requirements mapping can be complex. Evaluation criteria can be more general than specific, and sometimes Section L instructions will have no evaluation criteria against them. The PWS may not have a direct correlation with the proposal instructions. RFPs can have errors, especially draft RFPs, with sections referenced that are missing or mislabeled. Some instructions can be interpreted multiple ways depending on the wording. For these reasons, if your team is using AI to help map requirements, it is imperative that you check the mapping manually early on that satisfies the RFP response criteria and then maintain a version you know is correct.

Most proposal teams use a compliance matrix or annotated outline as a tool for tracing every instruction to a destination in the proposal. This helps proposal management and reviewers check that nothing is missing, nothing has been duplicated unnecessarily, and nothing has shifted out of sequence along the way by well-meaning AI edits or formatting.

2. Volume Requirements and Formatting Rules

Is the template compliant with RFP formatting requirements?

Each proposal volume is usually a self-contained system with its own requirements, page limits, and formatting parameters defined by the RFP. These rules are not suggestions. Assume that all volume requirements will be scored by evaluators. Exceeding a volume page count usually means that any pages over the limit will not be read. Volume instructions may dictate margins, font sizes, file types, and pagination.

Most AI tools do not inherently enforce these formatting rules. The editor must review each volume for alignment to submission instructions, validate headers, footers, volume starts, and digital submission formatting.

3. Terminology and Labeling Consistency

Are solution terms consistent with the RFP?

Terminology in proposals is not interchangeable. To an evaluator, changing a heading from "Program Management Plan" to "Project Delivery Overview" may seem careless or even non-compliant. AI often paraphrases to improve variations in narrative, but in compliance, fidelity is paramount.

Label every heading, table, and figure exactly as it appears in the RFP unless explicitly instructed otherwise. Deviations can distract the reviewer and suggest either misunderstanding or negligence. You can prompt your AI to help you check that keywords are consistent throughout a document, but ultimately it is the editor that needs to verify proper use of terms.

4. Required Attachments and Certifications

Have all required deliverables been accounted for?

Appendices, attachments, and certifications may be required in your proposal submission. Many of these elements live outside Section L, appearing in Section J or embedded in RFP attachments.

These often include completed forms, past performance matrices, teaming agreements, licenses, representations and certifications, and any compliance checklists. Additional requirements need to be accounted for in your compliance matrix and cross-referenced to applicable proposal sections. AI tools may not know these requirements exist when tasked to create a response, unless prompted or explicitly trained to incorporate them. It is your job to track and confirm each one is accounted for.

5. Evaluation Criteria Alignment

How will the solution response satisfy scoring criteria?

While Section L gives you the required structure, Section M describes how the proposal will be scored. This is where proposal science meets subjectivity. Your proposal must not only be compliant, but also persuasive in the terms the evaluator will score.

Ensure language and keywords align with scoring criteria. If Section M rewards low risk, the team should reinforce risk mitigation strategies in applicable volumes and sections. If it emphasizes team qualifications, you'll need to decide how and where to highlight staff credentials, experience, and capabilities so they won't be missed.

ChatGPT and similar applications can help you check that evaluation criteria are satisfied and even suggest ways to incorporate logical responses. This is one of those areas, however, where AI content can overreach to try to satisfy the criteria by offering services, tools, or activities that are not actually part of your team solution. It can easily misinterpret the meaning of the evaluation criteria. It can apply examples that don't really fit. It can come to a conclusion based on hallucinated or erroneous data.

Similar to the GAO calling out contractors for submitting protests based on AI-generated hallucinations, untrustworthy proposal content generated by AI is going to be a topic that persists in the years ahead. It is essential that editors question AI content and engage SMEs to verify accuracy whenever there is doubt.

> **As of October 2025, the Government Accountability Office (GAO) has published nine protest decisions that have referenced non-existent or fabricated information and has called out protest filers for submitting "AI hallucinations multiple times."**
>
> (Wilkers, Ross. 2025. "Think AI Can Write Your Company's Bid Protest? Think Again." Washington Technology, October 14, 2025.)

Not surprisingly, there are several available applications that evaluators can use to check for AI-generated content. One of the better tools is GPTZero. Using this tool, one simply copies and pastes text into a window, presses a button, and the tool will tell you what percentage was likely created by AI and highlight those sections.

Expect that government evaluators will use assessment tools like GPTZero to gauge the degree of AI-generated material in a proposal and check sections with high percentages more closely.

6. Chapter 3 Quality Checklist: Editing for Compliance

☐ Map each Section L requirement to a specific location in the proposal.

☐ Ensure all evaluation points in Section M are addressed with matching language in the response.

☐ Review content for evaluation criteria keywords and flag any solution content or conclusions that should be verified by SMEs.

☐ Cross-reference Section C technical tasks with response content as required by the RFP instructions

☐ Verify formatting rules including font size, margin width, headers, footers, and pagination are followed.

☐ Check that every volume begins as instructed and includes any required verbiage, separators, or tabs.

☐ Ensure correct RFP terminology is represented in headings, tables, and attachments.

☐ Review for contradictory or unclear RFP references that need clarification.

☐ Update the compliance matrix throughout the review process and share with volume leads.

☐ Verify inclusion and proper labeling of all required attachments and forms (for final check).

☐ Check that file types, digital signatures, and submission platforms are in compliance (for final check).

7. AI Training Tips: Improving Compliance Outputs

SETUP TIPS

- Paste Section L and Section M directly into your prompt before requesting content.

- Ask AI to preserve exact language from headings and task statements when building outlines.

- Include a sample compliance matrix as part of your AI's reference material.

- Provide a list of formatting rules (page limits, font, file type) in the setup instructions.

- Use a tracked checklist prompt to ensure attachments and appendices are recognized and referenced.

PROMPT EXAMPLES

Compliance Outline Prompt

Using Sections L and M, generate a detailed response outline with exact RFP language for all headings. Include mapping references.

Instruction Mapping Prompt

List each item in Section L and identify where it should appear in the proposal, including section numbers and intended page counts.

Formatting Prompt

Review this document against the following formatting rules and list any violations by page number.

Attachment Prompt

List all forms, appendices, and certifications required by this RFP and where they should appear in the final submission.

Evaluator Focus Prompt

Highlight where this proposal addresses each criterion in Section M using matching terminology.

Chapter 4: Verifying Data

Verifying Metrics, Names, Sources, and Past Performance Data

Throughout an RFP response, data serves as the measurable evidence that lends weight to claims and helps orient evaluators to your firm's credibility and capacity to perform. Without accurate data, even the most eloquent prose becomes suspect. Editors must therefore serve as the stewards of truth with a skeptical mindset to fact check and validate data that might have been generated by AI.

Editors reviewing material that contains AI-generated content must be twice as diligent as they have been in the past. Managers should allocate twice the hours for editors to complete their reviews and ask questions to verify content. For all the time proposal teams will be saving by using generative AI, this should not be a strain on business development budgets.

We can't assume that any data is factual unless it is traceable to a reputable source. Your division leads, authors, or SMEs may have used AI to generate data to save them time. One mistake is enough to instill doubt for those evaluating the proposal, and they may question other parts of the submission that would have otherwise been trusted. Even after a contract award, a serious misrepresentation in the proposal will come back to haunt the awardee. Verifying the data preserves the integrity of the submission, which is the reason this chapter is probably the most important in the handbook.

1. Spotting Hallucinated or Fabricated Content

Is it real?

Until confirmed by someone who knows, every data point in a proposal is a hypothesis, especially when content providers have access to AI tools. AI is capable of synthesizing text that appears deeply logical and technically convincing at first glance. But it can insert metrics, cite performance data, or list project outcomes that never happened. This phenomenon (known as AI hallucination) poses a serious threat to the credibility of the proposal. Your role as editor is to examine each piece of data and ask, "Is this real?" and "Is the reference appropriately sourced?"

The editor must verify where a number originated, how it was measured, and whether it is relevant to the contract and relevant to the context of the section. In particular, be aware of any:

- Numbers generated without units of measurement

- Numbers, dates, or timelines presented that do not add up properly

- Statements like "We improved system performance by 47%" without a source citation

- A past performance example for a project that has not been approved for use or does not have documentation readily available to check against

- Names of people, projects, systems, or tools that are not well-known elements of the solution

Using an application like GPTZero to determine the likelihood of whether content was generated using AI will help prioritize the editor's time. But robot author or not, editors need to know that data presented has a reliable and traceable source.

2. Validating Dates, Timelines, and Durations

Do the dates and schedules add up?

Start dates, end dates, project durations, and compliance timelines must all be correct and not conflict with each other. AI may misalign these details by making guesses or by confusing projects in the library it has been fed.

Confirm that all project dates match what's listed in source documents like resumes, project summaries, or past performance references.

Make sure delivery timelines stated in the proposal conform to the schedules in the RFP or reflect a feasible implementation window based on the solution. Verify transitions, phase-ins, and milestones for logic and consistency.

If timelines seem off between the RFP instructions, the response, or in context of other contract activities, make sure that these are intentional discrepancies by confirming with the solution team. If mismatches are intentional or strategic, the narrative needs to clearly explain why a schedule is different than expected, and hopefully that explanation is one that benefits the customer.

3. Verifying Personnel, Titles, and Qualifications

Are they the right people with the right quals?

A simple AI error in proposing a key employee or their credentials incorrectly in a Federal procurement can be viewed as a material misrepresentation and can have serious consequences when it violates the False Claims Act (FCA) or the False Statements Act (18 U.S.C. § 1001).

The GAO has voided awards after the awardee proposed unavailable key personnel. The Department of Justice (DOJ) and agency inspector generals have pursued civil and even criminal cases for misrepresenting key staff on a contract.

AI may misassign titles or exaggerate credentials based on prior prompts, resumes, prior proposals fed as source content, or internal erroneous logic. If possible, compare each person's title and background to official resumes and HR data. Check that job titles and names are used consistently across the Technical, Staffing/Management, and Business volumes.

Editors must ensure that named personnel in the proposal are real, qualified, and available to work the contract. Speaking with the people proposed directly is the best way to verify information like this. If you don't have access, or if this activity is above your pay grade, make sure you have access to the person who can verify and approve this information, and then make a record of how and when personnel data was verified for the proposal. The legal team will thank you if a future grievance ever winds up in court.

Can you ask AI to verify these things for you? Yes, but then you still have to check the references it provides to see if they are real. AI may just give you a convincing false answer so it can go back to playing solitaire or whatever game it enjoys in the ether when it is not busy completing a task for you.

4. Cross-Checking Past Performance Claims

Did we really do this?

One of the most common and critical areas of error in AI-generated proposals is past performance references. AI that is not diligently trained and prompted may fabricate customer names, agency acronyms, contract values, or outcomes based on pattern recognition that fills in blanks with best guesses rather than reality.

Do not accept any case study or performance example from AI-generated content until it has been confirmed against reputable source data or by a senior contributor of the past performance contract in question. Past performance material that has been approved for submission on your bid will likely have plenty of support documentation, CPARS, or other published reviews and reports that will be helpful in verifying details. Contracts that are used as examples in the narrative that do not have this level of verifiable detail must be vetted for accuracy.

Confirm the project cited occurred with the participants stated or implied by the text. Validate dates, personnel, and performance claims, such as "delivered under budget" or "completed 3 months early," with internal reports, CPARS, or contract documents you can find. If someone on the team says something is true without offering a document or link for proof, make a note of that attestation and who said it. This is not just to cover your own rear, if you had a question about it, others will too, maybe even the government.

5. Ensuring Data Consistency Across the Proposal

Do you have a Wall of Truth for numbers?

Data does not live in isolation. Like information should appear consistently across the Technical, Past Performance, Management, and Cost volumes. If one staffing table says 27 FTEs and another says 32, the evaluator will doubt both numbers. The editor must compare key values, percentages, names, acronyms, and dates throughout all sections of the proposal.

A professional document uses standard units and formats throughout the proposal. If hours are used in one section and person-months in another, ask leadership which one they want to use, convert and normalize them, and then ask for verification from both volume leads. For example, decide whether to express percentages as 85% or 85.00% and apply that decision consistently. Do the same for weights, dollars, periods, distances, etc.

You can use your AI to help find measures and numerical formats mentioned throughout the proposal, however, instructing it to make changes automatically could cause errors that may go unnoticed. A better strategy is to verify numbers in a Wall of Truth document and feed that document to your AI to discover discrepancies.

6. Chapter 4 Quality Checklist: Verifying Data

- ☐ Verify all project names, dates, values, and durations match official documents or past performance references.

- ☐ Check personnel names and titles against resumes or HR source data.

- ☐ Confirm AI-generated metrics, statistics, and performance indicators are traceable and accurate.

☐ Cross-check past performance claims with CPARS, contract records, or internal reports.

☐ Make a note of attestations when questioned data is not readily provable.

☐ Verify accuracy of table bullets, steps, and tasks with SMEs.

☐ Ensure data presented in tables matches values mentioned in the narrative.

☐ Look for duplicate figures or conflicting numbers across volumes.

☐ Check all dates and timeframes against project scopes and transition plans.

☐ Standardize how metrics and units are expressed throughout the proposal.

☐ Flag any vague values or overly rounded estimates for review.

7. AI Training Tips: Getting Better Data Outputs

SETUP TIPS

- Provide source documents such as resumes, project summaries, and compliance matrices before asking the AI to generate content.

- Use fact-labeled inputs. For example, include data that you know is factual like "Project A: $4.5M, completed 2022, CPARS score 4.8/5" before your prompt or as an attachment.

- Prompt the AI to flag any data it cannot confirm or explain or recommend alternatives based on known facts you provide.

- Feed the AI prior proposals, performance narratives, or other relevant documents and reports to replicate style, tone, structure, and substantiated data.

- After verifying correct numerical values in a Wall of Truth, feed it to your AI as a source for checking numbers in the response.

PROMPT EXAMPLES

Data Accuracy Prompt

Create a new MS Word file and for each claim in the following draft, insert a comment highlighted in yellow if a metric or value cannot be verified by the RFP or the project documents already provided.

Timeline Generator Prompt

Using the attached staffing plan and schedule, generate a delivery timeline that includes realistic phase-in, execution, and hand-off periods that is compliant with the RFP.

Past Performance Prompt

Based on the data below/attached, generate a past performance narrative that includes agency name, value, duration, objective, and outcome. Include specifics that are relevant to the RFP section X. Do not invent any details.

Cross-Check Prompts

Review the following proposal sections and list any discrepancies in staffing levels, labor categories, cost figures or implied cost, and delivery milestones.

Review the following proposal sections and identify any similar values that are measured or formatted differently, e.g., weights, dates, cost, time. In general, weights should be shown in metric tons, dates should include a day, month, and year, costs should be shown in dollars with commas and no decimals and abbreviated with M for millions or B for millions when exceeding 999,999. Create a separate MS Word file that includes and highlights all identified discrepancies in yellow. Highlight any of your comments in yellow also.

Placeholder Flag Prompt

Scan this text and identify any placeholder numbers, values, references, or estimates that should be verified before submission. Create a separate MS Word file and highlight findings and your comments.

Chapter 5: Editing Tables

Making the AI's Tables Reader-Ready and Evaluator-Friendly

A proposal table can affirm or weaken credibility in a glance. Tables provide a good way to display data that is fixed, structured, and easy to read.

AI is good at making tables and reorganizing information based on confirmed data points. If you decide to use AI for only one thing, this is that thing: sorting numerical data, listing risks and mitigations, comparing topics across similar attributes, and describing steps to an established process. However, when AI generates tables, it may do so without concern for human scanning patterns or evaluator intent. As an editor, your task is to check for congruence, clarity, and consistency to these visual arguments.

This chapter explores how to review, refine, and standardize tables created by AI so that they convey useful, scorable content.

1. Aligning Table Content to Narrative Claims

Is the content relevant and data rich?

When AI is told to make a table, it's going to make a table. That doesn't mean it has value. If a table appears without context, or presents values never mentioned in the prose, it can be a disruption rather than support.

The editor should check that the detail provided is valuable and scorable for this section. Does it properly prove claims made in the introductory paragraph, or could the entire table easily be replaced by a short paragraph?

On the other hand, sometimes a table is exceptional and relevant, but the surrounding narrative fails to describe its relevance. Ensure each table is introduced, cited, or explained in the surrounding text to justify its purpose. Every table should reinforce a point made in the narrative that helps satisfy a requirement.

2. Verifying Table Bullets

Is every bullet valid and true?

AI-generated tables are often so convincing on the first draft that people stop inspecting them for accuracy after reading a few rows. The editor doesn't have this luxury.

AI can invent content or pull data from unverified sources if not specifically trained on a limited dataset. It may reiterate content in multiple ways unnecessarily to fill out the space (e.g., it decides three bullets per cell is mandatory output).

It's important for editors to have access to solution leads when reviewing tables like these to make sure each bullet is relevant, not redundant, and that proposed steps are actually in scope for the contract. These are some questions the editor needs to ask:

- Will they hand this list of activities to a worker to perform or is it just a convenient answer for the proposal response?

- Is this a process or tool we are proposing for the contract? If so, is it represented in other sections, like the cost volume?

- Are these the correct people or positions responsible for these actions?

- Is this bullet valuable, or does it mean the same as a previous bullet?

- Does the data referenced make sense in context of the work scope we're addressing in this section?

- Do the features and benefits noted actually provide client value for this contract?

Ideally, SMEs will be available before Red Team to review table content for their area of expertise. Tables with a wide range of content should have multiple reviewers who are each assigned a priority (such as technical accuracy, benefits statements, software or hardware specifications, personnel roles, etc.) to focus their attention on bullets.

3. Improving Readability, Layout, and Terminology

Can it be better?

A good table uses the fewest columns and rows necessary to communicate the intended message. Overly dense tables can overwhelm the eye. AI can output unbalanced or unnecessarily windy tables because it does not really understand the objective or the subject at hand.

The editor should be enabled to:

- Simplify and cut content where possible and group related data for space efficiency and clarity.

- Use approved templates to edit for consistent alignment, spacing, captions, and headers.

- Change cases to be consistent. Engineers often capitalize too many words and some AIs copy that odd habit.

- Define acronyms and spell out abbreviations.

Tables should persuade as well as inform. Check for visual emphasis that draws the evaluator's attention to differentiators, strengths, and low-risk indicators. Engage proposal management for how to format emphasis like bold text or shaded cells.

Table headings, just like section headings, should match the language of the RFP whenever possible. If the solicitation instructions use the term "Contract Number," do not label the column "Contract ID." Editors should confirm all headers are unambiguous and that titles reflect evaluator expectations. The editor should also verify tables comply with formatting instructions for presenting content.

Be on the lookout for a table that is just a frame around converted content from narrative text or a set of bullets. Evaluators may see this type of table as an attempt to avoid narrative format restrictions like font size or page limit, e.g., "just throw this page of text into a table to save page count." If that is in fact the contributor's intent, consider other types of data or additional columns that would add value to make the table more informational.

4. Ensuring Cross-Table Consistency

Is it similar to other tables in the response?

Sometimes proposal contributors are working in a vacuum and may not know that a similar table has already been created in a previous section. If so, that's an opportunity to combine tables and refer back to save space.

Staffing numbers, labor categories, dates, and metrics presented in tables must match what appears in the narrative and across volumes. Even slight discrepancies—like a staffing plan that shows 24 FTEs while the cost volume shows 26—can reduce evaluator confidence. Use the checklist in Chapter 4 to make sure data appearing in tables are consistent between them.

Table formats should already be standardized in the proposal template for use as a go-by. As work progresses, editors should work with production staff to update styles to accommodate new table structures or formats not yet covered by the template. Bullet styles and tone should be similar, at least across the same volume. Are you using periods at the end of bullets in a table or not? Does the font, spacing, color, and text alignment across the volume look like it came from the same document?

A lot can change between Red Team and the final submission. With contributors using AI to help them provide content in a pinch, the editor should cross-check all tables before submission, even if they have done it in previous reviews. Using the compare document tool in MS Word, or engaging AI to do something similar, is a good idea to see if there are brand new tables that haven't been thoroughly reviewed since Red Team.

5. Chapter 5 Quality Checklist: Editing the Tables

- ☐ Confirm that each table supports a claim in the surrounding narrative.

- ☐ Verify accuracy of table bullets, steps, and tasks with SMEs.

- ☐ Make a note of attestations when table content in question is not readily provable.

- ☐ Ensure tables are cited, introduced, or explained before or after their appearance.

- ☐ Check that headers match RFP terminology and are consistently formatted.

- ☐ Simplify overly complex tables—reduce unnecessary rows or columns.

- ☐ Use uniform fonts, cell padding, and alignments for cleaner visuals.

- ☐ Verify visual emphasis (bold, shading, grouping) follows proposal guidelines.

- ☐ Cross-reference staffing numbers, metrics, and dates with other volumes.

☐ Avoid repeating the same table structure with slightly different content—consolidate where appropriate.

☐ Ensure embedded tables do not exceed page limits or formatting constraints.

6. AI Training Tips: Helping AI Format Better Tables

SETUP TIPS

- Provide AI with examples of well-structured tables that have been used successfully in past proposals.

- When commissioning a table from AI, include instructions for the number of columns, preferred labels, and whether to include totals or summaries.

- Add formatting instructions such as: "keep to under 6 columns," or "fit to 6.5 inches wide using 10 pt Times New Roman."

- Flag common table types in your organization (e.g., past performance, staffing matrix, risk register) so AI can reuse successful formats.

- When Section L specifies the table content requirements, provide the instructions to the AI and verify its interpretation

PROMPT EXAMPLES

Staffing Table Prompt

Generate a staffing table showing each labor category, number of FTEs, and project phase. Include total FTEs and cross-reference this with narrative estimates.

Past Performance Table Prompt

Create a table summarizing the three relevant past performance contracts from attachment X. Include customer, scope, value, duration, and key outcomes.

Risk Register Prompt

Build a risk register table addressing the attached workplan with columns for risk description, likelihood, impact, mitigation steps, and residual risk. List the risks in order of high impact to low impact.

Graphics Placeholder Prompt

Suggest areas and types of supporting graphics related to complex content mentioned in table X could provide relevant clarity and help evaluators score this section.

Format Enforcement Prompt

Reformat this table to combine the last two columns, ensure equal row spacing, and align all numerical data to the right.

Chapter 6: Editing Graphics

Reviewing AI-Enhanced Visuals for Accuracy and Message Impact

It was novel when people first started using AI to create comical memes and photos with seven-fingered celebrities in unlikely settings. It was also somewhat reassuring that these images were obviously AI-generated. Pictures contained scrambled or nonsensical letters. Perspectives were a little off. Charts and graphs were more representative than they were vehicles for displaying actual data. This is changing fast.

Proposal graphics have always been used to help display data efficiently and illuminate processes that words alone cannot convey. A well-placed visual can lead the reviewer to an important message quickly and effectively. The editor's role has historically been to ensure that graphics support, reinforce, and clarify the accompanying narrative, as well as adhere to proposal formatting standards. As AI is becoming more capable of generating graphics based on appropriate training, the editor will soon have to assume that all graphics are AI generated and therefore adopt a skeptical eye to evaluate graphic content. This chapter explores how to review and revise graphics in AI-assisted proposals.

1. Ensuring Visual Clarity and Accuracy

Is the graphic scorable in support of requirements?

Every diagram, chart, or workflow should be scorable and add value to an RFP response. AI may create attractive visuals, but it may also label things incorrectly, misalign processes, depict outdated concepts, or just miss the mark in terms of adding value in the right place.

The editor should review each visual for technical correctness, confirm labels match the narrative, ensure logic flows from left to right or top to bottom when appropriate, and verify each element has a clear function. Graphics must adhere to solicitation guidelines for usable typefaces and type sizes and must be scaled to fit within proposal page limits. Where applicable, confirm branding (logos, icons, imagery, etc.) aligns with your organization's standards.

Most importantly, when AI has been used to generate a graphic, the editor needs to ask:

- Does the graphic add scorable value to the section by supporting a proof or explaining how your firm meets relevant requirements?

- Can the Volume Lead or a SME attest to the origin and accuracy of all data presented in the graphic?

2. Verifying Alignment with Narrative Content

Does the narrative support the graphic?

Proposal graphics should not stand alone like some do in books, articles, or periodicals. They must be embedded within a context that tells evaluators why the visual matters so that they are scorable.

The editor should review how each graphic is introduced in the narrative (figure callouts introducing the graphic should appear before the graphic), how it is explained, and whether it directly ties to a section-relevant customer requirement, objective, or evaluation criterion.

Graphics with many steps or details warrant some discussion in the text to focus reviewers on the most important elements. The reason for the graphic should also be evident by the caption. Does the caption clearly convey its purpose? Does it include a customer objective or benefit? If not, the editor should ask the contributor what the best conclusions would be in displaying the graphic for their section. There are SMEs that focus entirely on graphics and spend little time thinking about text. Others are the opposite and may barely inspect an AI-generated chart for relevance, satisfied that they have some decoration on the page. In either case, the editor's job is to care.

3. Graphic Copyright and Traceability

Can we use this graphic?

There are legal concerns to consider in AI graphic generation. In the past, dealing with copyrighted imagery was simpler. If you found a graphic you liked from a third party or competing party that you did not have rights to, you could design your version differently, change the content, verbiage, and customize the look, feel, or emphasis of the graphic enough to avoid copyright infringement.

With AI-generated graphics, image sources are not obvious. AI art may be original enough to use out of the box, or it could be an exact copy of a vendor's proprietary process graphic. How would you know?

The best answer is to prompt the AI to only use a company-owned dataset and to provide examples of graphics that you know will not have copyright issues. Contributors who use AI to generate any content need to get into the habit of logging their prompts and sources for the benefit of the team and their firm to help avoid legal troubles.

As an editor, if you don't have access to how the graphic was made, there are some things you can do. Again, this requires more of your time than a traditional proposal edit. You can perform web searches for images on the topic or title and see how close you are to finding a similar graphic on the first page. For example, if your Scaled Agile Framework graphic looks exactly like the standard process graphic from Scaled Agile, Inc. (and they are not on your team to approve the image use) then you have successfully identified an issue.

If the graphic references a capability rating from a third party, check that rating against published material from the third party. Most industry market reviewers, like Gartner, have strict rules on how you can display their data.

Many winning federal proposals are available to the public after award, so image rights do matter. If you don't find a correlating graphic popping up on a Google search, that doesn't mean you're completely safe, but you should continue to remind proposal management, contributors, and your legal department that due diligence is expected when initially generating AI artwork, so that graphic investigation becomes less of an issue going forward.

4. Reviewing Common Graphic Types

Checks by graphic type.

Different visuals serve different purposes. The editor should be familiar with the types of graphics typically found in proposals and how to evaluate them. Below is a list of what to look for specific to common graphic types:

- Process Diagrams – Check for a logical flow, that arrows make sense, and that steps conclude as expected.

- Organizational Charts – Ensure roles, names, and titles match the proposal's staffing section and anywhere else roles are mentioned.

- Infographics – Evaluate whether data presented is accurate and enhances understanding for reviewers about the topic at hand.

- Icons and Callouts – Make sure icons are not overdone or too obscure and that callouts reinforce key messages without cluttering the layout.

5. Eliminating Redundant or Ineffective Graphics

Is the graphic effective?

The editor should assess each visual for clarity and purpose. Graphics should aid the evaluator in understanding your approach to meeting requirements and providing value on the contract. Sometimes a graphic introduces confusion because the content is too tangential or the text does not justify the graphic's placement. If a graphic does not add value, it should be removed or replaced with something better.

Sometimes a graphic merely repeats what has already been addressed in the text. In this case, decide if the graphic should stay or if the full text should stay, or if either should be edited for space.

The proposal instructions (Section L) often provide hints about what type of graphic would be relevant in a particular section by the verbiage used in the requirement. If instructions contain the word "How," a process or framework graphic may be appropriate. "When" implies some type of schedule. "Where" could be a physical or functional map. "Who" may imply an organization chart or responsibility matrix. "Why" might warrant a case study or industry graphic to explain your rationale. "What" could be a capability infographic or a proposed architecture diagram. If the graphics presented in a section don't seem to be addressing the who-why-when-what-where-and how from the instructions, the editor should question their validity in the response.

6. Graphic Editing

Most AI-generated graphic content is not (as of yet) easily editable using traditional software platforms. Your AI may be able to make edits based on your direct instructions, but it may also make other changes that you did not ask for, which means you need to review the entire graphic after each revision assisted by AI.

An alternative is to use AI-generated backgrounds for your graphics and overlay text in another program. You can do this with Adobe Illustrator, MS PowerPoint, and several other applications to maintain control of the content and lower risk of AI changing already approved data or verbiage.

Stay tuned for software companies to provide AI graphic solutions that are easier to edit for use with RFP responses and other types of business publishing. Because the technology is new and advancing quickly, it's a good idea to save graphics in standard formats, including png, jpeg, pdf, ai, and ppt, to make sure your graphic files outlast any company or special formats that could vanish through acquisition or attrition.

7. Chapter 6 Quality Checklist: Editing the Graphics

☐ Confirm all graphics are accurate, clearly labeled, and relevant to the proposal content.

☐ Ensure every visual is cited or referenced in the surrounding text.

☐ Check that messaging is consistent with text and caption, providing reviewers value labels that are easy to score.

☐ Check flow directions and consistent layouts within process flows.

☐ Verify compliance with solicitation rules on file type, font use, and size limits.

☐ Ensure visual branding aligns with company and template guidelines and is consistent across graphics, including typefaces, lines, colors, and styles.

☐ Replace or remove AI-generated visuals that are off-topic, generic, or poorly rendered.

☐ Validate acronyms, metrics, and labels for technical accuracy.

☐ Ensure diagrams and icons are legible and at a quality resolution in print and onscreen.

☐ Avoid duplicating visuals that serve the same explanatory purpose.

☐ Review all elements in graphics that have been revised using AI, not only the changes.

8. AI Training Tips: Improving Graphic Use with AI

SETUP TIPS

- Provide the AI with prior proposal visuals that were well received.

- Describe what each visual is intended to communicate before asking AI to generate content.

- Embed graphic placeholders in your outline to signal where visuals should go and what they should depict.

- Clarify any formatting rules such as DPI resolution, color schemes, or labeling requirements.

PROMPT EXAMPLES

Graphic Planning Prompt

Suggest three types of visuals that would enhance this section. Explain the purpose of each graphic.

Workflow Diagram Prompt

Generate a step-by-step process diagram for our transition plan. Include labels and brief callouts.

Compliance Visual Prompt

Check whether the following images meet the RFP's rules on page format and labeling. Suggest revisions.

Icon Placement Prompt

Insert visual cues or icon labels to emphasize differentiators in the following section.

Narrative Tie-in Prompt

Write a paragraph that introduces and explains the graphic shown below. Connect it to the evaluation criteria.

Chapter 7: Editing Prose

Fixing AI Weaknesses: Repetition, Vagueness, and Voice Drift

When your author is a machine, it can generate language that is vague, repetitive, and brimming with unnecessary fluff. Editing an AI author requires more attention to voice. Your AI lacks the self-conscious discrimination usually earned by human writers during middle-school shaming experiences. It doesn't know when it's awkward and it doesn't know when its assertions or conclusions are gratuitous.

As a result of the rising use of consultant-speak and legalese in the early 2000s the U.S. government passed the Plain Writing Act (PWA) of 2010 (https://digital.gov/guides/plain-language) to help make information more accessible and understandable for intended audiences and the public at large. The PWA is worth a revisit now that AI is creating content and can be used as a source for creating style rules (see prompts section below for suggestions). There are also writing styles and sentence constructions that suggest ChatGPT was used to write a paragraph, which can frustrate your evaluator and damage the trust you're trying to establish.

AI-generated content should never go straight to a Red Team review. AI can save writers and SMEs a lot of time in developing section responses, but editors will need more time to incorporate AI-related checks into their reviews. For best results, response teams should include editors earlier in the development process so they can ask participants questions and review any AI-generated material for discrepancies as it is produced.

In this chapter, we explore what to look for, what to revise, and how to train AI to do better next time when drafting the narrative.

1. Removing Repetitive or Empty Phrasing

Is the narrative repetitive?

AI models tend to repeat language patterns, resulting in a paragraph filled with repetitive structures: "Our approach is proactive. We offer a proactive solution. This proactive strategy ensures..." Many editors already hear a voice narrating content as they read. If you're more of a visual learner than audio learner, reading aloud may help you catch repetitive or awkward phrasing quicker than scanning text alone.

ChatGPT loves to use transitional starting words repeatedly including "Additionally," "Furthermore," "Moreover," "However," etc., and the more they appear on a page, the more obvious it is that they are not necessary.

ChatGPT also has a habit of saying the same thing using different words within the same paragraph. Editors should assume they will need to combine sentences that are redundant and eliminate sentences that are just taking up space without contributing substance. This is especially important for page-limited documents.

2. Eliminating Vague and General Statements

Is the text generic?

One of the most common signs of AI-generated content is vagueness. Phrases like "industry-leading," "robust solution," or "tailored approach" that are overused by human authors are now going to be suspected of AI generation because they are vague descriptions that lack substance. Evaluators who are already wary of reviewing AI-generated material are going to see through generalizations and expect specificity and credibility.

Editors should try to replace these placeholder statements with real data, examples, or qualifications. Turn "robust" into "designed to support 250 concurrent users with 99.99% uptime." Turn "tailored" into "configured specifically for the Department's hybrid cloud infrastructure."

Another give-away is the dramatic or philosophic general opening statement that sounds like it was pulled from an early 20th century dissertation, such as, "Customer satisfaction remains the touchstone by which every call center measures its soul." Any opener that feels like it is being presented in an amphitheater while sporting a stiff collar and tails was probably AI generated.

There are already numerous applications that analyze texts for AI content. So far, we've found GPTZero to be more effective than others we tried, but this technology will change rapidly along with every other AI-related tool. All the products we tested made mistakes in identifying AI vs. human generated text. From this day forward, even if you never use AI to generate proposal content, you may be accused of it anyway because of vague or generalized statements in your proposal narrative.

3. Correcting Passive Constructions and Grammar Drift

Is the narrative more active than passive?

AI favors passive voice if not prompted otherwise, as if they were trained on the passive tense prevalent in technical manuals. Excessive use of passive constructions makes a proposal feel distant and impersonal. Phrases like "the solution will be implemented by our team" should become "our team implements the solution."

Editors should also watch for shifts in tense, point of view, or mood throughout the document. An AI evaluator may not care about these shifts, but these inconsistencies can disorient a human reader. Consistency in grammar, tense, and perspective helps keep an evaluator reviewing without pause.

4. Restoring Human Voice

Does it sound autogenerated or salesy?

AI can produce sentences that are emotionally unconvincing. Some of this is due to a bland or risk-averse tone. Sometimes it's just verb use.

AI narratives undercut confidence with words like "can/may" instead of "does/will." "Can" or "may" are words sometimes used for legal reasons in a solicitation response, but they should not be prevalent in describing the results of your approach. The editor should look for ways to strengthen claims that are likely to be true. For example, "Our solution may improve service delivery during startup," should be "We improve service delivery by integrating the X process on Day One."

Proposals need a tone that is assertive and professional to maintain a reader's confidence, without being too salesly. ChatGPT in particular will slip in exaggerated marketing language when it runs out of hard data, presumably from training on commercial sites and documents.

To establish a solid argument and control salesy narratives, the editor should identify claims throughout the text and look for details and proof points nearby to substantiate those claims. If the team can't back up a claim generated by AI, then you need to cut the unsubstantiated claim so it doesn't harm your score.

To reduce suspicion of AI-generated text (whether or not AI has been used), the editor should look for other common signs of AI-generated text including:

- **Generic or simplified claims.** "Our approach ensures efficiency, transparency, and impact." Replace broad claims with more specific statements about why the approach is efficient, what makes it transparent, and exactly what kind of impact we're talking about. A generic sentence that could apply to almost any topic is not adding value to the narrative.

- **Overuse of antithesis statements or negative contrasts.** For example, "Our objective is to identify systemic errors and determine root cause, *not to merely fix symptoms*..." A phrase like this using negative contrast in the same sentence can be flagged as AI, especially if the construct appears several times in the same section.

- **Overuse of em dashes.** Em dashes used to be cool. Now they're a red flag for AI-generation. Use them sparingly.

- **Overuse of lists.** AI is good at making lists. Lists are not always useful in the middle of a paragraph, though, especially if there is an opportunity to use story telling. For example, "The team will analyze data, generate insights, produce reports, and support decision-making," sounds more human when presented as a series of activities using a variable rhythm, such as, "Our lead analyst runs the weekly data to generate insights based on current and cumulative trends. Then he pushes findings to the management office system to automatically build and deliver reports, enabling the leadership team to make timely decisions based on real data."

- **Conclusions using the word "both."** For example, "This process is both efficient and effective." It's the overuse of simple constructs like these that make them so suspicious. Quantifying the efficiency and effectiveness based on past performance, analysis, studies, etc., is the best way to make a claim like this believable. For example, "This process has doubled delivery capabilities while reducing labor costs by more than 50% on similar projects, like X and Y."

5. Shaping Paragraphs for Readability and Logic

Is there a good story flow?

Without proper training, AI-generated paragraphs often lack a logical flow. Editors should check to see if paragraphs that introduce sections follow a clear progression. For example: a claim statement that satisfies a requirement; evidence that proves the claim; what the impact will be for the customer.

Other worthwhile readability edits include:

- Breaking big paragraphs that look like a wall of text into two or more paragraphs.

- Finding opportunities to add callouts, bullets, subheadings, or graphics to make reading blocks of text less tedious.

- Reviewing the logic of how one topic relates to the next topic in the same section. A paragraph that seems unrelated to the one right before it may need a transition statement, or, both topics could be introduced in an introduction paragraph to justify their placement.

6. Chapter 7 Quality Checklist: Editing the Prose

☐ Remove repeated words, phrases, and sentence patterns.

☐ Identify repeated adjectives or sentence openings (e.g., "proactive," "additionally," "moreover").

☐ Combine redundant sentences expressing the same idea in slightly different words.

☐ Eliminate filler or "echo phrases" that restate an idea without adding substance. Replace vague language with specifics—metrics, actions, systems, or timelines.

☐ Flag generic phrases that could apply to any company or solution.

☐ Check that claims are substantiated with evidence.

☐ Remove dramatic, academic, or "philosophic" openers that sound performative rather than factual.

☐ Revise passive voice into active voice when it improves clarity.

☐ Ensure consistent use of tense and point of view across sections.

☐ Replace hedging terms ("can," "may," "typically") with assertive verbs ("will," "does," "enables") when claims are supportable.

☐ Remove exaggerated or marketing-sounding phrasing when it lacks technical grounding.

☐ Reduce AI tells like generic triads, and overuse of em dashes, excessive lists, repeated antithesis, etc.

☐ Check for human rhythms—does the paragraph read naturally, or does it sound algorithmic?

☐ Break long paragraphs into smaller, scannable sections, or suggest other ways to interrupt walls of text for readability (e.g., subheads, bullets, charts, callouts, quotes).

☐ Ensure narrative complements any tabular or visual content.

☐ Review content against PlainLanguage.gov guidelines for clarity, brevity, and audience focus.

☐ Reduce legal jargon or consultant-speak unless it is well defined.

7. AI Training Tips: Improving Prose Output

SETUP TIPS

- Provide sample paragraphs with ideal tone and structure as prompt references.

- Request varied sentence structure and reduced passive voice.

- Feed examples of language that includes metrics, data, and named tools.

- Flag phrases you never want to see (e.g., "cutting-edge," "synergy") so AI avoids them.

- Ask AI to simulate voice consistency by aligning tone to an organization's published materials.

- Use an AI detector like GPTZero to evaluate current AI prose (AI Detector - Free AI Checker for ChatGPT, GPT-5 & Gemini).

PROMPT EXAMPLES

Tone Cleanup Prompts

Revise this content for stronger, more confident tone. Replace vague phrases with specifics. Maintain formal voice.

Revise text using an active voice using first-person plural (we, our team) where appropriate.

Revise confident verbs ("will," "enables," "delivers") rather than hedging terms ("may," "can," "typically").

Words and Symbols to Avoid Prompts

Avoid filler transitions like "additionally," "moreover," or "furthermore" unless they are contextually needed.

Avoid words that could be legally binding in context of the statement including "ensure" and "guarantee"

Avoid use of Em dashes in the narrative

Active Voice Prompt

Convert passive constructions to active voice while preserving meaning and technical accuracy.

Fill in the Details Prompt

Replace vague adjectives (e.g., "robust," "industry-leading") with quantifiable metrics or examples.

Paragraph Logic Prompt

Restructure the following paragraph using the format: claim → evidence → expected result.

Confidence Language Prompt

Identify uncertain or weak language (e.g., may, can, generally). Suggest firmer alternatives. *Note: words like "may" and "can" will sometimes be used intentionally for legal reasons depending on context, so it's important these words are not auto-replaced within a document.*

Voice Alignment Prompt

Rewrite this section to match the tone of our past performance summary: direct, precise, credible.

Plain Writing Act Prompts

Write in plain language as defined by the Plain Writing Act of 2010 and the Federal Plain Language Guidelines. Always:

- Lead with the main point and organize for the reader.

- Use active voice, present tense where possible, short sentences (aim ~20 words), short paragraphs that describe one idea, and everyday words.

- Use lists, headings, and tables to make information easy to find.

- Remove fluff, legalese, and duplicative wording.

- If technical terms are required, define them briefly first.

- If the user requests a more formal tone, still comply with the rules above.

Before replying, self-check against a plain-language checklist and revise. If requirements conflict, state the trade-off for word replacement.

Self-Editing Prompts for the AI

Scan this draft for repeated words or phrases and consolidate redundancy.

Identify and rewrite any vague statements lacking data or examples.

Review for tone consistency: confident but not salesy, professional but approachable.

Chapter 8: Cross-Section Editing

Ensuring Consistency, Continuity, and Cohesion Across the Entire Proposal

A proposal is a set of interconnected parts that should reinforce each other. Similar to humans working in a vacuum, when AI generates content from isolated prompts, we see fragmentation occur between sections in the response. Numbers may shift. Terminology drifts. Similar claims across volumes may contradict each other. It is the editor's responsibility to unify these threads into a coherent, credible whole, which is only possible when reviewing across volumes.

In the old days, teams performed cross-section reviews on a wall in the war room as authors generated their content. Remote work has put more of that burden on the proposal management team, especially on the editing staff. AI generated content adds even more complexity to the challenging effort of checking that all parts of the submission are consistent and complementary.

This chapter guides you through the practice of scanning across sections and across volumes, comparing parallel sections, and resolving inconsistencies before they reach the customer.

1. Standardizing Terminology Across Volumes

Are terms used consistently?

Every term, acronym, and phrase used in the proposal should carry consistent meaning throughout. AI tools may describe the same system in multiple ways or alter job titles subtly between staffing and technical volumes. If the Management Volume refers to a "Cybersecurity Analyst" and the Technical

Volume calls them a "Security Lead," the discrepancy could raise doubts about whether they are the same person.

Ideally, you can build or reference a terminology glossary and verify each instance where terms are reused in a Wall of Truth that is accessible by the entire team. You can also feed the Wall of Truth to your AI to help you identify parallel terms.

Many firms have established corporate style guidelines for proposals. If you notice AI content has broken a corporate guideline, there's a good chance it has happened more than once. You can use AI to help check against these guidelines, either one prompt at a time or by feeding it your style guide for finding exceptions in the response.

2. Verifying Data and Metrics Across Sections

Does the data match?

One of the easiest ways to lose evaluator confidence is to submit mismatched data. If a table in the staffing plan describes 15 labor categories and the Business Volume budget shows 12 categories, the proposal appears rushed or inconsistent. If the same metric is presented in minutes in one section and seconds in another, it needs a correction.

The first step when finding a discrepancy is to check if the RFP references a similar category or metric. If not, the team needs to make a call and then communicate the decision to all contributors who use the same data.

The editor should cross-validate all staffing levels, budgets (FTE mentions), measures and metrics, dates on schedules, and deliverables data across sections. The proposal manager should make a list of responsible content leads who can quickly make decisions or collaborate on the correct response. Any data appearing more than once in the proposal should also be added to the Wall of Truth.

These cross-section data checks should happen at least twice with the editor involved. Once before Red Team (first draft review), and once before Gold

Team (final draft review). If the team is using AI to help recover from Red Team, we can't assume that data values haven't changed.

3. Reinforcing Win Themes and Strategic Messages

Is the message clear?

A strong proposal reinforces its win themes consistently across volumes. If "low risk transition" is a theme, we would expect it appear in the Executive Summary, Transition Plan, and Management Approach. If past performance is a firm strength, there should be references to past performance in the Technical Volume that are traceable to Past Performance Volume.

The beginning of every volume should mention at least two major strengths or discriminators to help guide evaluators. Ideally, there will be other sections in the volume where those themes can be repeated and supported with evidence.

By reviewing across volumes, the editor can weigh the strength of win theme and strategic messaging use in different sections. Some contributors will be very aware of messaging, and some not at all. The editor should note where strategic messaging would apply to weaker sections and include examples of where other sections have strong related content for the section lead.

4. Aligning Section References and Cross-Links

Is the reference correct?

Proposals often include references like "see Section 4.2" or "as described in the Management Plan." These pointers must be checked for accuracy, especially if the section referenced could impact the score.

Page numbers and section numbers change, sometimes on the very last day. Section titles and subtitles shift. AI generated content may have hallucinated references or used outdated section numbering. As editor, validate that every internal reference points to the correct location and label within the proposal.

If there are hyperlinks to internal or external documents, make sure they are permissible, and that they work as expected.

5. Ensuring Narrative Continuity and Tone

Is there a story to follow?

Sometimes the construct required in a proposal response doesn't lend itself to a compelling story telling format, which is OK; proposals are more often scored than read like a book, especially if the evaluator is AI. But where there is an opportunity for a story, we might as well add it for the benefit of a human evaluator. Does the proposal as a whole have a single story? And is that story obvious in the Executive Summary and echoed in the Technical Volume? Does the Executive Summary seem to overpromise based on the response in other sections or volumes?

Check if the tone and content evolve naturally and cohesively from start to finish for each volume. The editor should also look for abrupt tone shifts, duplicated content, or gaps in logic between sections describing the same topics. Do the Technical and Management Volumes provide evidence that supports the overall story? Are there strong proofs mentioned in volumes that should also be mentioned in the Executive Summary or volume introduction?

6. Chapter 8 Quality Checklist: Cross-Section Editing

- ☐ Confirm that key terms, job titles, and technology names are consistent across all volumes.

- ☐ Validate numerical consistency: staffing levels, cost estimates, schedules, and performance metrics.

- ☐ Verify that documents conform to corporate style guide.

- ☐ Ensure win themes and key messages are repeated and reinforced in multiple sections.

- ☐ Review all cross-references for accuracy in section numbers and titles.

- ☐ Check that acronyms are defined with first use per volume and used consistently.

- ☐ Eliminate content duplication that appears without added value.

- ☐ Confirm that past performance examples are consistent across narrative and summary formats.

- ☐ Ensure visual elements (tables, charts, captions) are referenced and labeled consistently.

- ☐ Standardize formatting between volumes for readability and visual unity.

- ☐ Read sequentially to identify tone shifts, contradictions, or narrative gaps.

- ☐ Standardize punctuation, grammar, and capitalization conventions.

7. AI Training Tips: Strengthening Cross-Volume Coherence

SETUP TIPS

- Feed AI outputs from one section into prompts for another to maintain consistency of message and structure.

- Feed AI the corporate style guide and Wall of Truth.

- Provide a centralized style sheet or glossary as part of every session involving multiple sections.

- Prompt AI to check for inconsistencies by summarizing values or headings used in related sections.

- Use prompts that ask AI to reinforce or reference points introduced in another volume.

PROMPT EXAMPLES

Glossary Consistency Prompt

Review this volume and confirm that all terms align with our glossary definitions. Summarize discrepancies.

Style Guide and Wall of Truth Prompt

Review this volume and confirm the narrative adheres to style guidelines document. Summarize discrepancies.

Review this volume and confirm that relevant data aligns with Wall of Truth document styles and terminology. Summarize discrepancies.

Metric Alignment Prompt

Cross-check staffing levels and cost figures between the following two sections. List inconsistencies.

Win Theme Integration Prompt

Identify opportunities to reinforce the win themes from the Executive Summary in this section.

Section Reference Prompt

Validate all cross-references (e.g., see section X.x) for accuracy and correct labeling and report discrepancies.

Narrative Coherence Prompt

Check for tone and content consistency between the Executive Summary and this section. Suggest adjustments to either document that could strengthen messaging.

Chapter 9: Self-Scoring the Response

Grading the Proposal Before the Government Does

Sometime before engaging executives to proofread the response at Gold Team, proposal management should pre-score the response. Create a simulated score sheet based on the evaluation criteria and in order of the Section L instructions. It may not be a perfect match to the government's score sheet, but it should be close based on the information provided in the RFP. AI can help you create the scoresheet. This simulated evaluation can reveal weaknesses that may have been overlooked, and may require SME input for revisions, so it's important to complete it before response teams are dismissed. Ideally, the scoring exercise should not be combined with other reviews or editing activities. You should not be critiquing writing style at this point. You should only assume the role of evaluator to score the documents.

This chapter describes steps to complete the self-scoring activity. AI may not inherently align narratives with evaluation logic unless prompted. Once the scoresheet is created and approved, the editor becomes the first evaluator, scanning with the criteria of Section M (with or without the help of AI) and asking: would this section response earn a top score?

1. Mapping Responses to Evaluation Criteria

Begin with Section M, the evaluation criteria. Understand how points will be awarded for each section. What are all the possible scores the government will have on its scoresheet implied by the RFP? If you know how the same customer has scored similar proposals, include that information in your criteria. What constitutes "Excellent?" What constitutes "Marginal?"

Refer to the compliance matrix you built from the RFP aligned with the response, as described in Chapter 3, and create a spreadsheet for each relevant section with your defined scoring possibilities. Add a notes column to your spreadsheet so you can explain why you scored each section the way you did.

You can feed your AI the solicitation, your compliance matrix, and the response to help you set up your scoresheet and to score each section. We recommend scoring the proposal yourself before looking at the answers from AI. Your analysis will likely have some differences.

Also, before feeding your AI any data, check again that your sharing settings have been turned off. Instructions for disabling data sharing in ChatGPT are included in the Introduction at the front of this book.

2. Simulating Evaluator Behavior

The goal is to evaluate the proposal as if you were sitting on the review panel. As an evaluator, you likely have a tight deadline, and you may be looking at many different sections from many different bidders. When you open the proposal, you're looking for a way to quickly decipher where to find the sections you need to score. As you read through the document, you're judging if you feel confident enough to give it full points, or if it falls flat. You may make notes so you can go back to a section before finishing your evaluation. You may open proposals from other bidders to compare responses between them for the same sections. And you may confer with colleagues on the details of the response before completing your evaluation. Ask yourself the following questions as you review:

- Was it easy to find the required content?

- Is the section worthy of providing full points? If not, what's missing or not convincing?

- If I'm not reading the perfect answer for this section, what would the perfect answer be for me as a customer?

Use your mock scorecards to simulate the scoring process according to the rules you understand apply. Flag any sections where you have doubts or need to discuss responses further with technical or management leads and content providers.

Then, look at how the AI scores the material. Your AI will sometimes surprise you with excellent points, and sometimes it will be way off the mark or misunderstand what is important in evaluating the response. Take the AI's best points and include them in your scorecard notes. Try to ignore any gratuitous flattery your AI gives you during the process.

3. Surfacing Strengths and Discriminators

Evaluators are required to justify high scores. We can help them by making strengths explicit in sections we think have excellent ratings.

Indicate opportunities to call out past performance, innovations, low-risk practices, and exceptional qualifications using focus boxes, tables, or other graphic elements that an evaluator can easily point to for justifying their score. Strengths and discriminators should be documented using language the evaluator can quote for a report or presentation

4. Identifying and Reducing Potential Weaknesses

Search for sections that may be scored down because of vague responses, inconsistencies, or missing elements. Weaknesses from a scoring perspective can be the result of incorrect assumptions in the response, filler language that doesn't serve to meet requirements or provide relevance to an approach, or unexplained decisions in the proposal that might actually have value to the customer if they included a rationale. Also, any response that is not obviously compliant after Red Team will need escalation. Flag these areas for immediate revision or strategic mitigation.

5. Communicate Your Score

Work with proposal management to finalize your scoring results. Management may have insights that clarify the response approach. They may also be surprised about weaknesses you've identified. The PM should decide how to distribute scores to the proposal team for immediate consideration.

It's prudent to maintain a scoring log that shows where each evaluation criterion is addressed and how well. This document can support internal review and justify last-minute edits. It also builds a historical record that can inform future bids or debriefings.

6. Chapter 9 Quality Checklist: Self-Scoring the Response

☐ Review Section M and highlight each scoring criterion in the RFP.

☐ Map proposal sections directly to the evaluation criteria.

☐ Use language from Section M to frame responses and highlight alignment.

☐ Simulate the scoring process using mock evaluator score sheets.

☐ Confirm strengths are clearly stated, quantifiable, and evaluator-visible.

☐ Eliminate vague, generic, or unsupported claims.

☐ Address any known weaknesses through mitigation language or additional explanation.

☐ Create or update a self-scoring matrix or score justification log.

☐ Use peer review to compare interpretations of the scoring outcome.

☐ Validate the proposal positions the offeror as low-risk and highly qualified in every scored area.

7. AI Training Tips: Enabling Self-Scoring Analysis

SETUP TIPS

- Include Section M in the prompt (directly or as an attachment) when generating or reviewing content for scoring alignment.

- Feed the AI previous scoring matrices and evaluator language to use as models.

- Ask AI to rate how well each section meets a particular criterion and to suggest improvements.

- Use prompts that require clear evidence of strengths or justifications for scoring.

- Simulate evaluator reviews using role-play prompts such as "You are a reviewer scoring this section..."

PROMPT EXAMPLES

Scoring Simulation Prompt

Act as a government evaluator using Section M. Read this section and assign a score with justification.

Criterion Matching Prompt

Identify where this draft addresses each evaluation criterion. Note anything missing or unclear.

Strength Visibility Prompt

Scan this section and highlight strengths that could be cited in the evaluator's comments.

Weakness Mitigation Prompt

List possible scoring weaknesses in this text and suggest ways to reduce or offset them.

Score Matrix Prompt

Create a table that lists each scoring factor and summarizes how it is addressed in the proposal.

Appendices

Appendix 1: Proposal-specific AI Product Review

Appendix 2: Useful Resources

Appendix 3: Prompt Engineering Logic

Appendix 1. Proposal-specific AI Product Review

Proposal Pilot

by Turingon

While putting this book together we had the opportunity to test an AI tool called Proposal Pilot, developed by Turingon.

Most large consulting firms that provide government products and services have been developing their own AI tools for years. Many of them began with ChatGPT and continue to customize their own internal platform with prompts and company document training to reduce time and improve data quality for their own proposal efforts.

Proposal Pilot is an AI-enabled response platform and fine-tuned LLM that is tailored to federal RFP language for compliance-driven drafting. Unlike generic AI writing tools, Proposal Pilot is designed explicitly around the federal proposal lifecycle, from solicitation ingestion and compliance mapping through Pink Team drafts, using collaborative editing and controlled iterations.

Turingon has offered their AI proposal development platform and support to clients similar to how consulting firms offer their proposal management processes and templates, and they are now offering various levels (Standard, Pro, and Enterprise) of the Proposal Pilot platform for use as an independent tool for proposal teams.

Product Highlights

The platform was developed by a team of experienced proposal managers, capture managers, writers, and SMEs, which is evident when examining the product's architecture, workflows, and guardrails (agent-based hallucination guardrails with outputs that are cross-checked against source documents before being surfaced to the user). Three product features stood out for us:

Solicitation-aware outline and draft generation. The most obvious value to using Proposal Pilot is producing Pink Team-ready structures in minutes rather than days. This could also be true of using ChatGPT alone with the right prompts, however, Proposal Pilot's proposal-centered architecture eliminates much of the frustration of training and correcting a generic AI assistant that defaults to generating marketing sound bites rather than compelling evidence-backed arguments. Proposal Pilot is certainly more focused on answering the solicitation requirements, and is very good at accounting for FAR, DFARS, and CMMC compliance. Turingon estimates a time savings of 40% when drafting responses for color team reviews using Proposal Pilot. We think this is a conservative estimate for many procurement types.

Automated compliance matrix generation with human editorial control. The compliance matrix or master proposal outline is one of the most manual labors in proposal development. An error in the outline can present development risks that will persist throughout the proposal lifecycle. Proposal pilot is good at creating outlines aligning with solicitations and its human-in-the-loop workflows ensure users retain editorial control and accountability over the outputs.

Secure integration with existing content libraries. The Pro and Enterprise options integrate with SharePoint on a secure government cloud, allowing teams to safely leverage validated corporate content. Customer data is not used to train shared public models. The system is structured around proposal artifacts—volumes, sections, compliance requirements, and corporate data—rather than free-form text generation from the internet. Being able to track where data and claims are coming from in AI generated content is a big plus that can prevent sleepless nights.

Conclusion

We were happy to explore this product and even happier to know that proposal professionals are creating accessible AI solutions that help address many of the risks of using AI tools for proposal tasks that we mentioned in this book.

Proposal Pilot is probably best suited for teams already operating with defined proposal processes and are accustomed to working with a disciplined step-by-step content creation approach. This platform helps move the needle of AI-assistance from a "doubt-everything" toward a "trust-but-verify" tool level. The compliance checks are a nice feature. The platform support staff is proposal-savvy and responsive.

For proposal professionals who acknowledge that working with AI is inevitable but remain rightly skeptical of generic AI tools, Proposal Pilot provides a thoughtful GovCon-tailored option to accelerate RFP responses using a controlled development architecture.

This is exactly the type of product we'll be watching as AI evolves and we think it's one of the platforms that will be setting the pace for the proposal development industry.

For more information about Proposal Pilot, visit https://turingon.ai/plans

Appendix 2. Useful Resources

Communities & Professional Groups

APMP International. The Association of Proposal Management Professionals is tracking AI trends. https://apmp.org

Proposal Management Professionals on LinkedIn. Peer community for proposal writers and editors discussing AI tools. https://www.linkedin.com/groups/49527

Reddit: r/proposals. Community for proposal professionals to discuss AI, tools, and RFP work   https://www.reddit.com/r/proposals

AI Tools & Platforms

AutogenAI. Enterprise-level AI proposal and grant writing automation platform. https://autogenai.com

ChatGPT. Fill in content and website.

Claude. Fill in content and website.

Loopio, Proposal automation and knowledge management with integrated AI drafting. https://loopio.com

Gemini. Fill in content and website.

Grantable. AI-powered grant writing assistant for nonprofits and proposal teams https://grantable.co

pWin.ai. AI platform for federal proposal and capture management optimization. https://pwin.ai

Proposal Pilot. AI platform for proposal creation and management for government contractors and agencies with CMMC- and FedRAMP-aligned controls for data security, secure infrastructure, access control, and audit readiness. https://www.turingon.ai/

Proposify. AI-driven sales and business proposal generation. https://proposify.com

Responsive.io. AI-based RFP response automation tool for corporate teams. https://responsive.io

Unanet AI. Analytics and proposal management software for GovCon. https://unanet.com

Industry News & Insights

Federal News Network. Government contracting and technology news, including AI trends. https://federalnewsnetwork.com

Washington Technology. Covers federal IT, contracting, and AI innovation in proposals. https://washingtontechnology.com

Devex. Global development industry coverage including AI in proposal writing. https://devex.com

ICTworks. AI use in international development, grant writing, and digital governance. https://ictworks.org

Learn Grant Writing Blog. Covers grant and proposal AI tools and methods for professionals. https://learngrantwriting.org/blog

RFP360 Blog. Discusses RFP automation, AI-driven sourcing, and content reuse. https://rfp360.com/blog

Policy & Ethics

Plain Language Guide. Principals of The Plain Writing Act of 2010 from digital.gov. https://digital.gov/guides/plain-language

Stanford HAI (Human-Centered AI). Explores responsible AI development and implications for content creators. https://hai.stanford.edu

AI.gov. Official U.S. federal resource on artificial intelligence policy and strategy. https://ai.gov

OECD.AI Observatory. Global AI policy tracker including guidelines for responsible content use. https://oecd.ai

Horizon Europe AI Guidance. EU resource on AI ethics in research and proposal contexts. https://horizoneuropencpportal.eu

Podcasts & Learning Channels

The RFP Success Show. Podcast about proposal strategy and process improvement. https://therfpsuccessshow.libsyn.com

GovCon Giants Podcast. Covers government contracting, AI tools, and proposal success stories. https://govcongiants.com/podcast

AI Today Podcast. Explores real-world applications of AI including content generation. https://www.cognilytica.com/aitoday/

The Marketing AI Institute. News and podcast hub about practical AI adoption for content creators. https://www.marketingaiinstitute.com/blog

Appendix 3. Prompt Engineering Logic

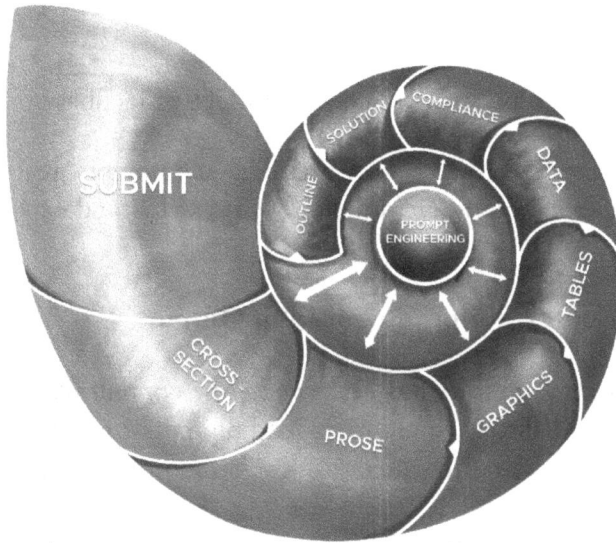

Prompt engineering has been described as the art of asking better questions. The more you practice creating prompts, the better you'll get at generating the types of responses that are helpful to you.

For the proposal editor, writing prompts becomes a supervisory act, similar to a proposal manager or volume lead supervising human authors. This appendix provides general guidelines and the overarching logic for designing prompts, regardless of the section, volume, or AI platform in use. Refer to the end of each chapter of this book for relevant prompt examples by response maturity.

1. Treat AI as a Junior Staff Member

AI is eager to please and will always attempt to produce something, even when it lacks sufficient context or verified data. It does not know when it is guessing, and it will not naturally ask clarifying questions unless instructed to do so. Effective prompt engineering therefore mirrors how an editor would brief a new hire:

- Define the task precisely

- Explain the audience and scoring logic

- Provide source material and boundaries

- State what not to do

- Review output critically and give corrective feedback

You should not expect AI to succeed with vague prompts, just as you would not hand a vague instruction to a junior human writer and expect a stellar result.

2. Establish Context Before Requesting Output

AI performs best when it understands where the content will live and how it will be evaluated. Editors should front-load prompts with contextual framing before asking for any drafting, analysis, or restructuring. High-value context typically includes:

- The proposal role the AI is playing (writer, evaluator, compliance reviewer, editor)

- The document location (volume, section, appendix)

- The evaluation lens (Section M priorities, risk sensitivity, scoring emphasis)

- The constraints (page limits, tone, terminology fidelity, formatting rules)

This context does not need to be repeated verbatim in every prompt, but it should be reinforced whenever the task changes. Without it, AI easily defaults to generic business/marketing writing rather than evaluator-focused proposal content.

3. Separate Thinking Tasks from Writing Tasks

One of the most common prompt engineering failures in proposal work is asking AI to analyze and create a draft simultaneously. These are different cognitive activities, and AI often performs them poorly when combined.

Editors should deliberately separate prompts into stages, such as:

- Analyze the requirement or problem

- List risks, gaps, or missing elements

- Propose structure or logic

- Draft narrative content

- Revise for clarity, revise for tone, or revise for compliance

This staged approach mirrors how experienced editors work. It also makes hallucinations easier to detect, because unsupported claims often emerge during the AI's analysis steps. Also, prompting to create content for one section at a time usually provides a better result (again, just like a human).

4. Constrain Language to Prevent Drift and Hallucination

AI has a strong tendency to embellish, generalize, and normalize content. Editors should explicitly constrain language and behavior through prompt instructions to reduce the potential fluff. Common guardrails include:

- Instructing the AI not to invent data, tools, or experience

- Requiring it to flag uncertainty instead of filling gaps

- Prohibiting paraphrasing of RFP headings or requirement language

- Limiting the use of stylistic fillers and abstract phrasing

The tighter the boundaries, the more usable the output becomes. However, as of the date of this book, we have yet to see a perfect paragraph flop out the other end of an AI prompt. Never assume the information you're getting from AI is true unless you know it to be true.

5. Reinforce Evaluator Logic Over Narrative Elegance

Generative AI is usually optimized for producing fluent, natural-sounding text. Proposal evaluators are trained to score responses against criteria. These objectives are not the same. Editors should continually redirect AI toward evaluator logic by emphasizing:

- Traceability to requirements for compliance

- Explicit "how" statements including who does what in a process

- Specific risk mitigations and controls

- Framing customer benefits aligned to the evaluation factors

6. Use Feedback Loops as Training, Not Correction

Correcting AI output once is useful. Correcting it in a way that the AI can generalize the instruction is more valuable. When revising AI-generated content, editors should explain why something is wrong, not just that it is wrong. Over time, this builds a working memory within a session that should improve subsequent outputs. Some effective feedback examples include:

- Compliance failures ("this does not map to Section L")

- Data risks ("this claim is unverified")

- Structural issues ("this belongs in another section")

- Tone problems ("this reads as marketing language, not technical")

Prompt engineering is iterative by design. Editors should expect multiple cycles and view each interaction as cumulative training rather than isolated correction.

About the Authors

Todd Hayes
Todd is a writer in Texas that has been contributing to RFP responses on major federal and commercial procurements since 1994. He has worked for a variety of leading firms to deliver more than 1,200 proposal products, resulting in $77B in contract awards. He has also authored several fiction and non-fiction works.

Robert Thompson
With more than 30 years of proposal and program management experience, Bob has managed and developed responses to RFPs of all sizes from small task orders to major programs valued up to $40 billion. Following a career in the U.S. Air Force. he performed as an evaluator for government source selection teams on major programs. He is also the author of multiple acclaimed history books.

Jilian Peeke
Jilian is a senior proposal consultant and technical writer with more than 25 years of experience developing compliant and responsive proposal content. She has led and written technical and management volumes across a variety of domains for government and commercial procurements, and is known for translating complex solution content into easy-to-score narratives.

Special thanks to John Ball for helping us edit this book.

To contact the authors with questions or comments, please send an email to info@kedwen.com with "When your proposal author is AI" as the subject.